I0042583

THE STATE OF URBAN FOOD INSECURITY IN CAPE TOWN

JANE BATTERSBY

SERIES EDITOR: JONATHAN CRUSH

Previous Publications in the AFSUN Series

Cover Photograph: Author

© *AFSUN 2011*

ISBN 978-1-920409-71-5

First published 2011

Production by Idasa Publishing, 6 Spin Street, Cape Town

CONTENTS

TABLES

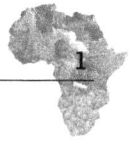

1. Introduction

Cape Town is the second largest urban area in South Africa, with a population now approaching 4 million.[1] The city is home to just over 7% of South Africa's population and had an average annual growth rate of 3.2% between 2001 and 2007, while the national growth rate was just 1.3%. Migration accounts for about 41% of the annual population growth of the city and natural increase the rest.[2] Although Cape Town contributes 11% to South Africa's GDP, the formal sector only experienced a 0.6% growth in employment between 2001 and 2004. Unemployment and poverty rates are increasing annually.[3]

As a result of its particularly rapid growth, the city faces a number of development challenges, including rising poverty, a housing backlog of 300,000 units and extensive urban sprawl.[4] The apartheid-era planning model consigned the poorest sections of the population to the periphery of the city. The legacy of this model is restricted access to the formal economy and a significant strain on urban infrastructure.[5] In addition, the national energy crisis and regional water scarcity may constrain future economic development.[6] These development challenges, together with the unsustainable spatial form of the city, have increased poverty and reduced food security for the urban poor of Cape Town.[7]

The relationship between poverty and food insecurity has been well documented in rural settings, including in the Eastern Cape from which many of Cape Town's migrants originate.[8] However, this relationship is not well understood in urban settings where poverty rates are high. The prevailing view is that food security in Sub-Saharan Africa is fundamentally an issue of improving rural food production, and that this will automatically resolve escalating food needs in urban centres.[9] In South Africa, the evidence shows that malnutrition rates are rising in urban areas, notwithstanding the fact that the country is nationally food secure and has a well-developed agricultural sector.[10]

South Africa's population is already more than 60% urbanised and is expected to reach 80% by mid-century.[11] Meeting the food security needs of the country's population is – and will be – an increasingly urban challenge. Addressing food insecurity in cities like Cape Town is therefore essential, not simply because access to food is a constitutional right but also because access to adequate, nutritious, hygienic and culturally-important food can assist the City's developmental aims.[12] The negative impact of food insecurity and hunger on individuals, and therefore on the places where they live and work, is well-documented.[13] The cumulative

impact of many undernourished individuals places significant limitations on the economic and social development of the city. Making the food system work for the poor can therefore have significant positive impacts on the economy, employment, environmental sustainability and health costs.

The African Food Security Urban Network (AFSUN) was formed in 2007 to address the challenges associated with rising poverty and food insecurity in the rapidly growing cities of Africa.[14] AFSUN's first major undertaking was to plan and implement a baseline urban food security survey in the SADC region. The survey was completed in late 2008 and early 2009.[15] This report presents the survey findings for Cape Town, focusing on the food insecurity of the city's poor communities. While income poverty is an important dimension of food poverty, the report also examines the influence of gender, housing and other household variables on levels of food insecurity in Cape Town. The report examines the food geography of Cape Town and the food sourcing strategies of poor urban households. Finally, it explores the relationship between food insecurity and health. The conclusion draws together the major policy questions that arise in relation to poverty and food security in Cape Town, with a view to providing an evidence-based platform on which to build future strategic responses to urban food insecurity at the metropolitan level.

2. METHODOLOGY

The AFSUN Urban Food Security Survey was conducted simultaneously in eleven cities in nine SADC countries: Blantyre, Cape Town, Gaborone, Harare, Johannesburg, Lusaka, Maputo, Manzini, Maseru, Msunduzi and Windhoek. The survey instrument was collaboratively developed by the AFSUN partners and utilized a series of food security assessment tools developed by the Food and Nutrition Assistance (FANTA) project including (a) the Household Food Security Access Scale (HFIAS) scale in which households are allocated to categories according to weighted responses to nine questions. The HFIAS scale provides an image of absolute access to food and access to appropriate food choices; (b) the Household Food Insecurity Access Prevalence Indicator (HFIAP) which groups scores on the HFIAS scale into four main categories: severely food insecure, moderately food insecure, mildly food insecure and food secure; (c) the Household Dietary Diversity Scale (HDDS) which asks what foodstuffs household members ate in the previous day. All foods are placed in one of 12 food groups, giving a maximum score of 12 and a

minimum of 0; and (c) the Months of Adequate Household Provisioning Indicator (MAHFP) which asks how many, and in which months, households had adequate food within the last year.[16] The survey also posed a further series of questions on household composition, income, housing, sources of food, migration and health.

The survey as a whole gathered data on 6,453 households and 28,771 household members across the SADC region. In Cape Town, a total of 1,060 households were surveyed in three poor areas of the city: (a) Ocean View; (b) Brown's Farm in Philippi (Ward 34) and (c) Enkanini & Kuyasa in Khayelitsha(Ward 95) (Figure 1). The survey was conducted in September and October 2008 using fieldworkers from the local community, the University of the Western Cape and the University of Cape Town. A total of 266 households were interviewed in Ocean View, 389 in Philippi and 394 in Khayelitsha.

These three different sites were chosen in order to capture any intra-city variations in the food security experience of the urban poor. Ocean View was founded in 1968 to accommodate Coloured households displaced by the Group Areas Act, and includes many households forcibly relocated during the apartheid era. The area has strong links to local fisheries which might impact on the food security of the population. Unlike the other two areas, it is also located close to wealthier suburbs which could provide additional job opportunities.

Brown's Farm (Ward 34) in Philippi and Ward 95 in Khayelitsha are both newer and rapidly growing areas. They attract residents from both rural areas and other urban areas in the city who move to obtain access to land, housing or employment. Ward 34 is located near to the Philippi Horticultural Area (PHA), a 1,500 hectare section of farmland surrounded by informal settlements. According to the Municipal Development Partnership for Eastern and Southern Africa (MDPESA), 60% of the PHA is under cultivation.[17] Although urban agriculture is a "marginal activity" in Philippi as a whole, MDEPSA and the Resource Centres on Urban Agriculture and Food Security Foundation (RUAF) feel that the area has considerable potential for urban agriculture. The choice of Brown's Farm for this study was influenced by the possibility of assessing the current and potential role of urban agriculture in household food security.

Enkanini & Kuyasa (Ward 95) in Khayelitsha is located on the periphery of the city and is predominantly populated by recent migrants to Cape Town. As there is a debate on the role of rural-urban links and migration in urban food security, Ward 95 was chosen because of the opportunity to examine the relationship between migration, rural-urban linkages and food security.[18] As this report demonstrates, there are indeed differences in the levels and determinants of food insecurity in these three sites. However, the local characteristics which led to the choice of these areas play less of a role in shaping food insecurity than other more general features of the urban environment that are common to all three areas.

FIGURE 1: Location of Survey Sites

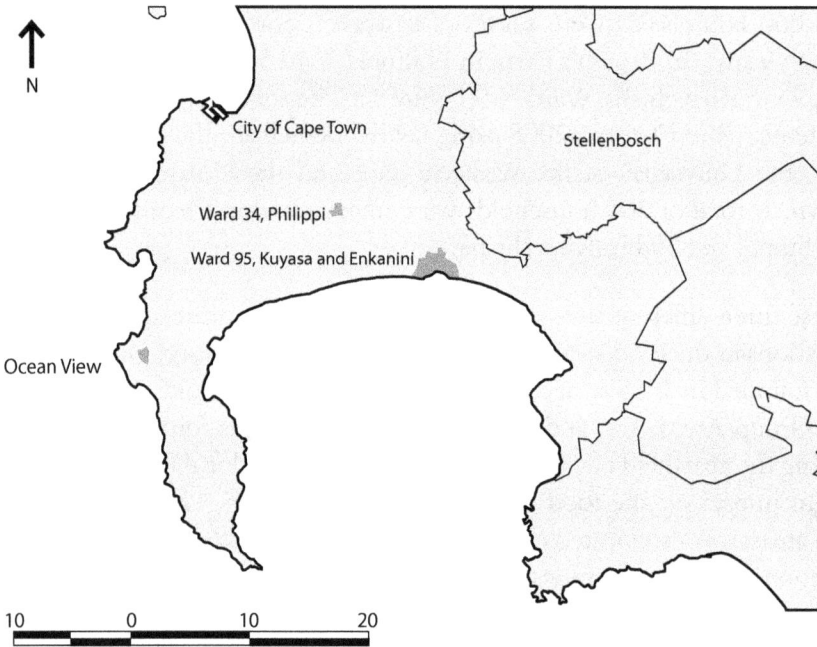

3. CAPE TOWN'S POOR: A POVERTY PROFILE

3.1 Household Composition

Female-centred households were the largest category of household in the Cape Town sample at 42% of all those surveyed. The second most important category was the nuclear family household (at 32%). The proportion of female-centred households varied, however, from 32% in Ocean View to 50% in Philippi (Figure 2). Ocean View was the only area which had more nuclear than female-centred households. The area also had a greater proportion of extended family households than the other two. Extended family households were the largest on average, with a mean size of 5.9.

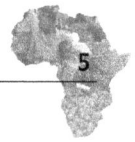

Male-centred households were the smallest, with a mean size of just 3.0. Over a quarter (27%) of male-centred households were single-person households (compared to only one in ten female-centred households). This can be attributed to the length of establishment of settlements, with the population of Khayelitsha consisting of many recent migrants, who are often single adult males. Single-person households were more prevalent in Philippi and Khayelitsha than in Ocean View.

FIGURE 2: Household Structure in Cape Town Study Areas

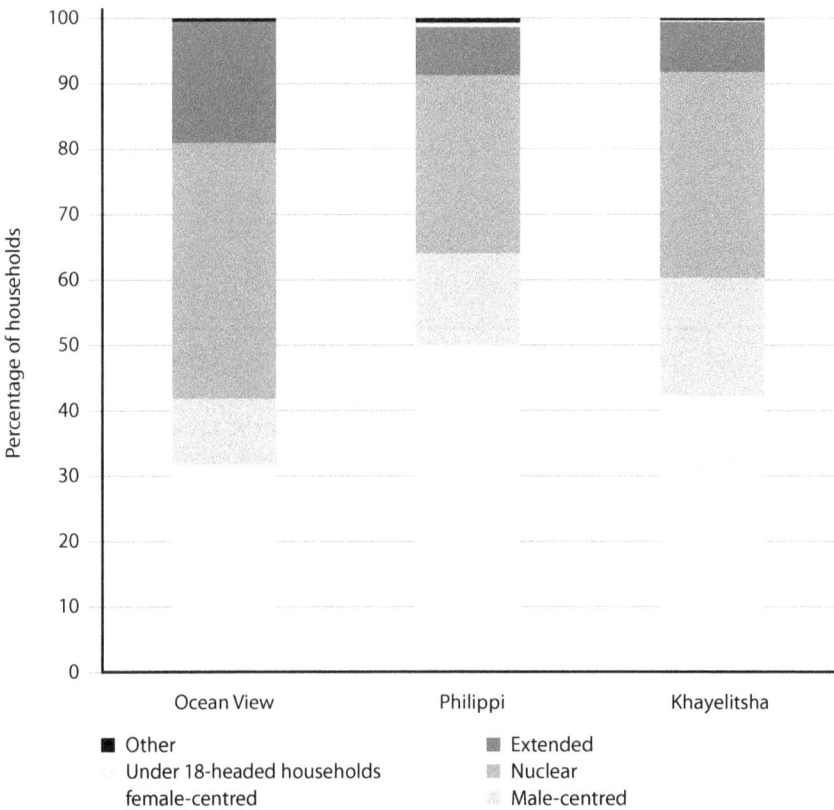

The mean age of the members of the surveyed households was 27 years. However, there was considerable variation from area to area (Figure 3). Ocean View (the oldest of the three areas) had a mean age of 31 and a mean age of 52 for household heads. In Philippi, the figures were 26 and 46 respectively, and in Khayelitsha (the newest of the three areas), they were 23 and 40. In other words, the more established area of Ocean View has a generally older population profile than the newer settlements in Philippi and Khayelitsha.

FIGURE 3: Mean Age of Sample and Household Heads

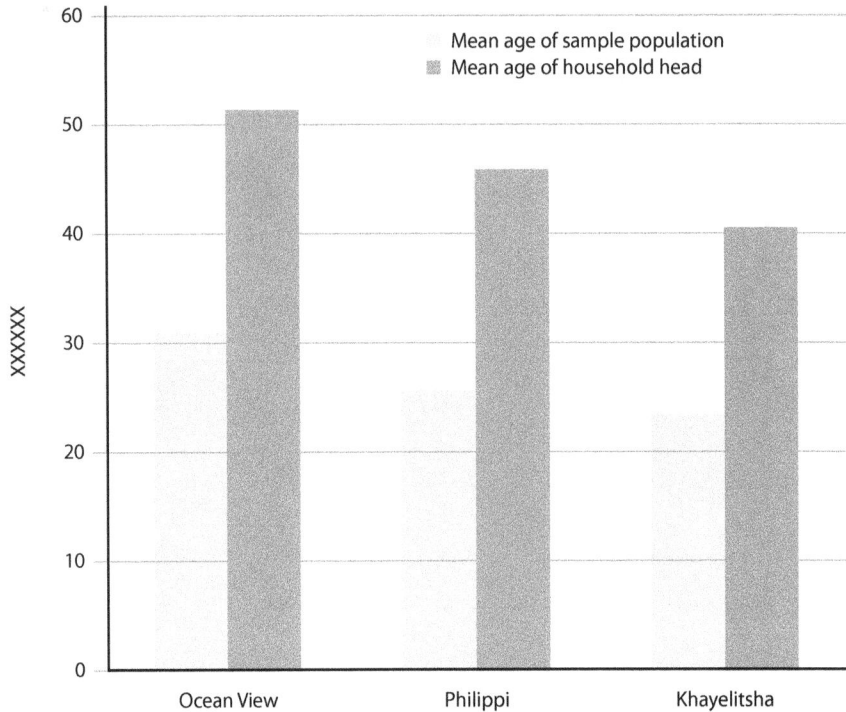

Associated with the different age profiles of the three areas were significant differences in their migrant composition. Only 4% of the population of Ocean View were rural to urban migrants, compared with 58% of Philippi residents and 62% in Khayelitsha. On the other hand, the relative importance of intra-city migration varied from a high of 52% of Ocean View's sample population to 28% of the population in Philippi and 21% in Khayelitsha.

3.2 Employment and Unemployment

Wage employment is the primary source of household income in the three communities. However, only 52% of the total working age population were working full or part time (Table 1). Nearly half (48%) of the working population were therefore unemployed. The unemployment rate did vary from area to area: Ocean View had the lowest unemployment rate (at 38%) while in both Philippi and Khayelitsha around 53% of the population was employed. The primary reason for this difference is geographical. Ocean View is located adjacent to several wealthy suburbs (Noordhoek, Fish Hoek and Glencairn) where there are better employment prospects. Philippi and Khayelitsha, on the other hand, are a significant distance from sources of wage employment. The apartheid urban model of racial separation and locating black South Africans on the periphery of the city

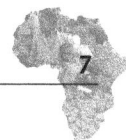

appears to still impact upon the ability of households to access the urban job market.

TABLE 1: Unemployment Rates in Study Areas								
	Total		Ocean View		Philippi		Khayelitsha	
	No.	%	No.	%	No.	%	No.	%
Employed	1101	52.4	419	61.9	347	46.2	335	46.9
Unemployed/Unpaid	1042	47.6	258	38.1	404	53.8	380	53.1
Total	2143	100.0	677	100.0	751	100.0	715	100.0

The most common forms of employment were domestic work (19%), skilled manual labour (16%), unskilled manual labour (15%) and service sector work (13%) (Table 2).

TABLE 2: Occupational Breakdown in Study Areas				
	Total	Ocean View	Philippi	Khayelitsha
	%	%	%	%
Domestic Work	18.6	13.4	24.2	19.4
Skilled Manual	16.2	22.7	9.5	15.2
Unskilled Manual	14.7	20.0	11.8	11.0
Service Work	13.5	12.9	12.7	15.2
Security	7.0	1.9	10.1	10.4
Own Business	5.8	2.6	9.5	6.0
Office Work	3.4	5.0	3.2	1.5
Truck Driver	3.3	1.4	4.0	4.8
Informal Work	3.2	1.2	4.3	4.8
Professional	2.8	3.3	2.9	2.1
Farm Work	2.8	1.2	2.9	4.8
Fisherman	2.0	4.1	0.6	0.9
Civil Servant	1.9	1.2	2.0	2.7
Police/Military	1.7	3.6	0.3	0.9
Health Worker	1.4	2.1	1.1	0.6
Teacher	1.2	2.4	0.9	0.0
Manager	0.4	0.1	0.0	0.0
Total	1101	419	347	335

Only 3% had informal business/trading as their main occupation which suggests that the poorest households are not participating to any signifi-cant degree in the informal economy. The relative importance of each employment sector varied from site to site. In Ocean View, for example, the most common forms of employment were skilled and unskilled labour

(at 23% and 20% of the employed population) followed by domestic work at 13%. Although Ocean View was selected because of its association with the fishing industry, only 17 individuals (around 4%) were involved. The pattern differed in Philippi and Khayelitsha, where domestic work was the most common form of employment (at 24% and 19% respectively). This may be related to the higher proportion of female-centred households in these sites as domestic work is a highly gendered occupation. In general, employment in all three areas was dominated by low-skill, low-wage work. There was a smattering of teachers, health workers, civil servants and police but the numbers were small (less than 5% in total).

3.3 Alternative Livelihood Strategies

Households in poor communities often diversify their livelihood and income generating strategies.[19] In Cape Town, however, there is little evidence of significant diversification. In the study areas as a whole, for example, only half of the households had any livelihood strategies additional to their main source of income. The proportion with a diverse portfolio of strategies (three or more sources of income)was only 19% and only 2% had four or more sources of income (Figure 4). The most common additional livelihood strategies were casual labour (16% of all households), followed by self-employment at home (8%), marketing (5%) and renting out space to lodgers (4.5%) (Figure 5).

FIGURE 4: Number of Additional Livelihood Strategies (% of Households)

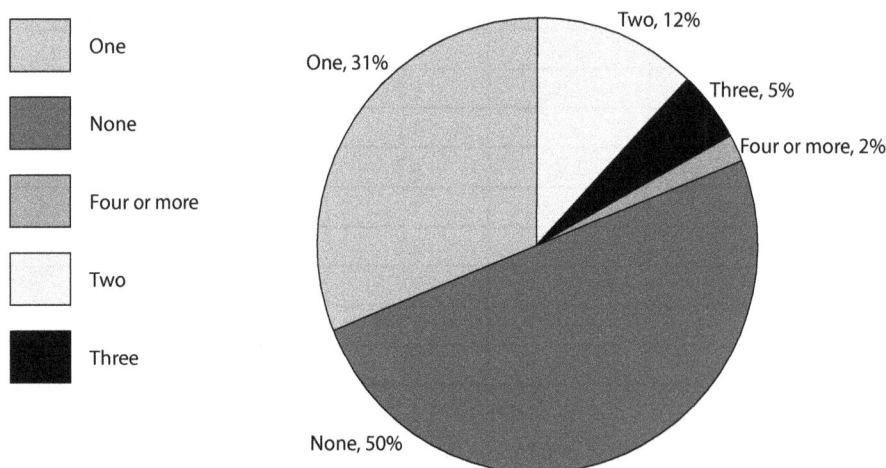

FIGURE 5: Types of Additional Livelihood Strategy

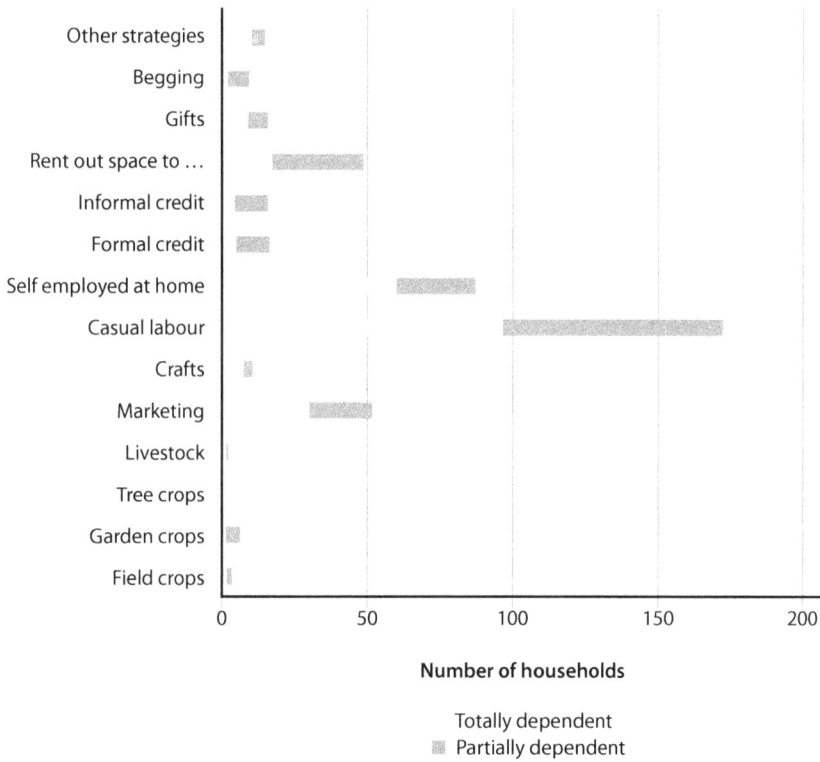

Number of households

Totally dependent
Partially dependent

What prevents poor households in the city of Cape Town from developing more diverse livelihood strategies? Does the scale and form of the city and urban governance shape the ability of households to diversify their livelihood strategies? When livelihood strategies are disaggregated by location some significant differences emerge. Some 27% of households in Ocean View rely on casual labour as an additional strategy, for example, which is around twice the proportion of Philippi households (14%) and almost two and half times the proportion of those in Khayelitsha (11%). The impact of the geography of the city can also be seen with regard to renting as an added livelihood strategy. There is a substantial housing shortage in Cape Town, particular in historically black areas. This shortage is informally addressed by households renting out rooms in their homes, or space in their backyards. The strategy is employed by 9% of households in Philippi, but less than 1% in Khayelitsha. With two-thirds of the sampled households in Khayelitsha living in informal shacks, the physical possibilities of renting are limited.

3.4 Household Income

The Western Cape Provincial Treasury estimates that nearly a quarter (23%) of Cape Town households earned less than R3,500 per month in 2009.[20] The City of Cape Town uses a figure of R2,800 per month to determine whether a household is indigent or not.[21] Three quarters of the households in the survey fell below the City's indigency threshold. Nearly a third of the total number of households reported incomes of less than R1,200 per month, 34% between R1,200 and R2,499 per month, and 34% over R2,500 per month. In other words, this report provides a picture of the food security situation of Cape Town's "bottom quarter" of households. Mean household incomes varied, however, from area to area in the survey: R4,499 in Ocean View, R2,197 in Philippi and R2,126 per month in Khayelitsha. In other words, in these communities themselves, the majority of households were below the indigency threshold.

Within the survey population, mean monthly income for employed men was R2,392 compared with just R1,874 per month for women. Female-centred households were most likely to be income poor (Figure 6). Forty-three percent of female-centred households fell into the lowest income tercile as opposed to just 19% of nuclear households. The more general reasons for the poverty of female-centred and female-headed households have been extensively discussed elsewhere.[22] They include unequal access to education and employment opportunities, the triple role of women in society (productive, reproductive and community management) and wider discriminatory laws and practices.

FIGURE 6: Household Income and Household Structure

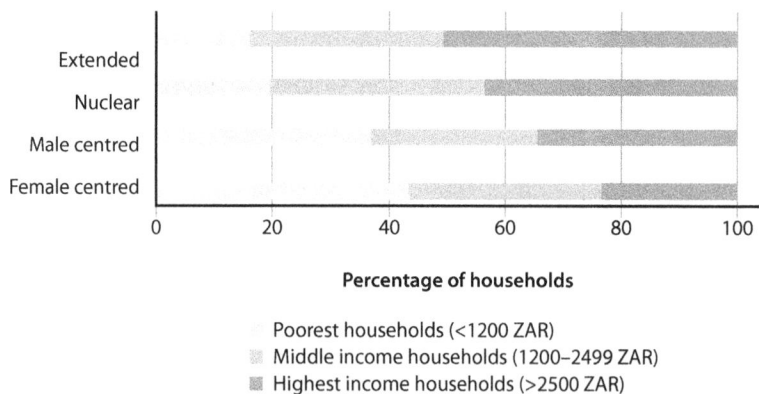

Percentage of households

Poorest households (<1200 ZAR)
Middle income households (1200–2499 ZAR)
Highest income households (>2500 ZAR)

The relationship between low income and unemployment was strongest in Philippi and Khayelitsha (Figure 7). The relationship was less strong in

Ocean View which had similar levels of unemployment but fewer house-holds in the lowest income tercile. The relationship between unemployment and level of education was strong in all three areas. However, the proportion of poorer households (those in the lowest income tercile) living in informal housing varied considerably, from a low of 10% in Ocean View to a high of 65% in Khayelitsha. It would be simplistic, however, to assume that those in informal housing are necessarily poorer than those who are not. Figure 8 compares the income terciles between shack and house dwellers, the two largest housing groupings in the survey. The differences between the two groups were not as stark as anticipated. The median declared income of the house dwelling households was R2,000, and that of the shack dwellers was R1,560. This is particularly interesting in light of the over-representation of formal housing in Ocean View, which would skew the data given the different income profiles of the three sites.

FIGURE 7: Relationship between Income, Unemployment, Education and Housing

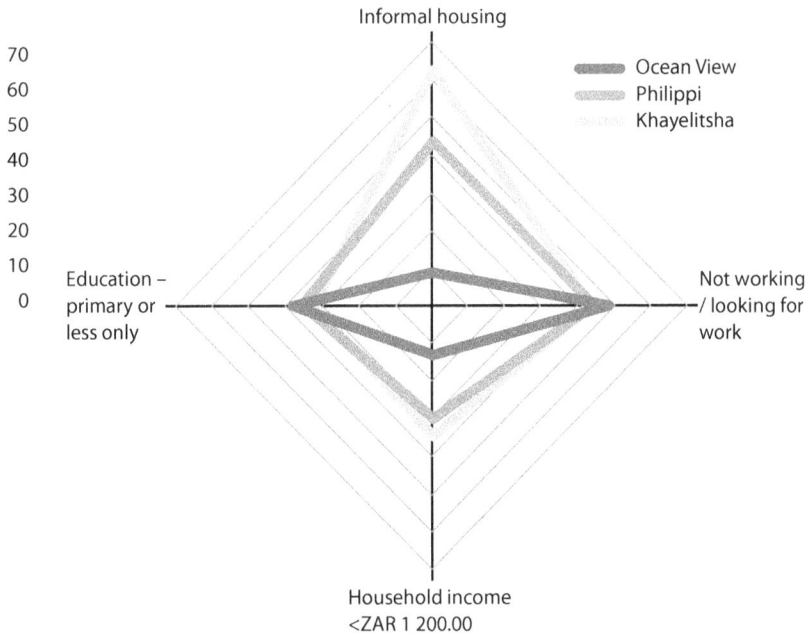

Source: 2001 Census

Figure 8: Income Terciles and Dwelling Type

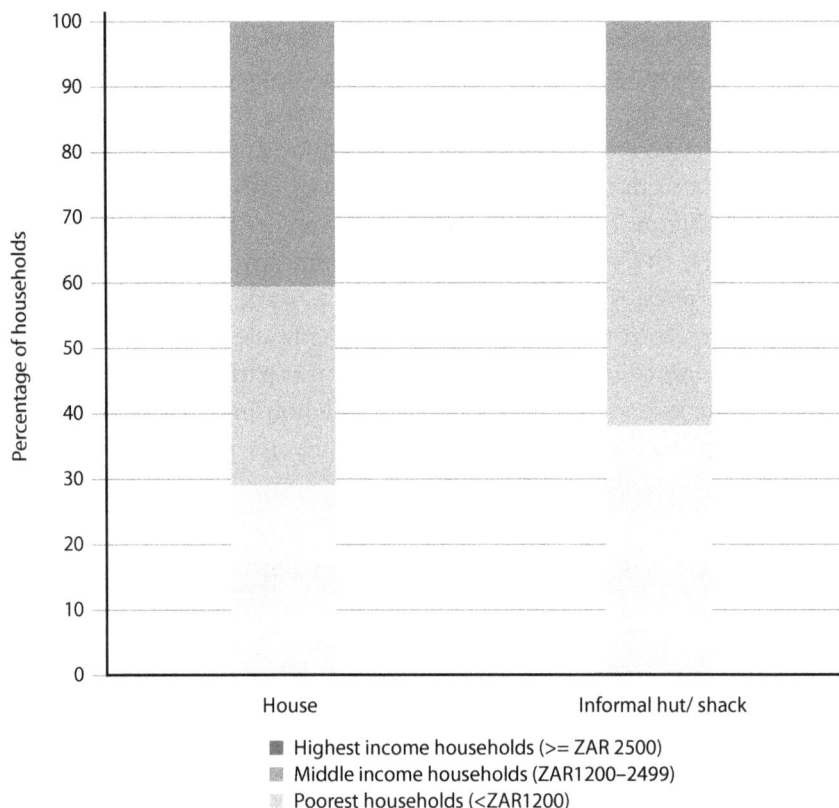

Highest income households (>= ZAR 2500)
Middle income households (ZAR1200–2499)
Poorest households (<ZAR1200)

3.5 Lived Poverty

The Lived Poverty Index (LPI) was used to measure aspects of the lived experience of poverty of surveyed households.[23] Households were asked how often they had gone without six key resources in the last year: (a) enough food to eat, (b) enough clean water for home use, (c) medicine or medical treatment, (d) electricity for their home, (e) enough fuel to cook their food, and (f) a cash income. The results were then calculated into an index score running from 0 (no lived poverty) to 4 (complete lived poverty, or constant absence of basic necessities). The mean LPI score across all sites was 1.01 (Figure 9), slightly higher than the South African average of 0.82.[24] The LPI scores were highest in Khayelitsha and lowest in Ocean View. The proportion of households with LPI's of greater than 1.0 was over 50% in the former and less than 20% in the latter. Across the city as a whole, 40% of households had scores of over 1.0 and 12% had scores over 2.0.

FIGURE 9: Lived Poverty Index Scores

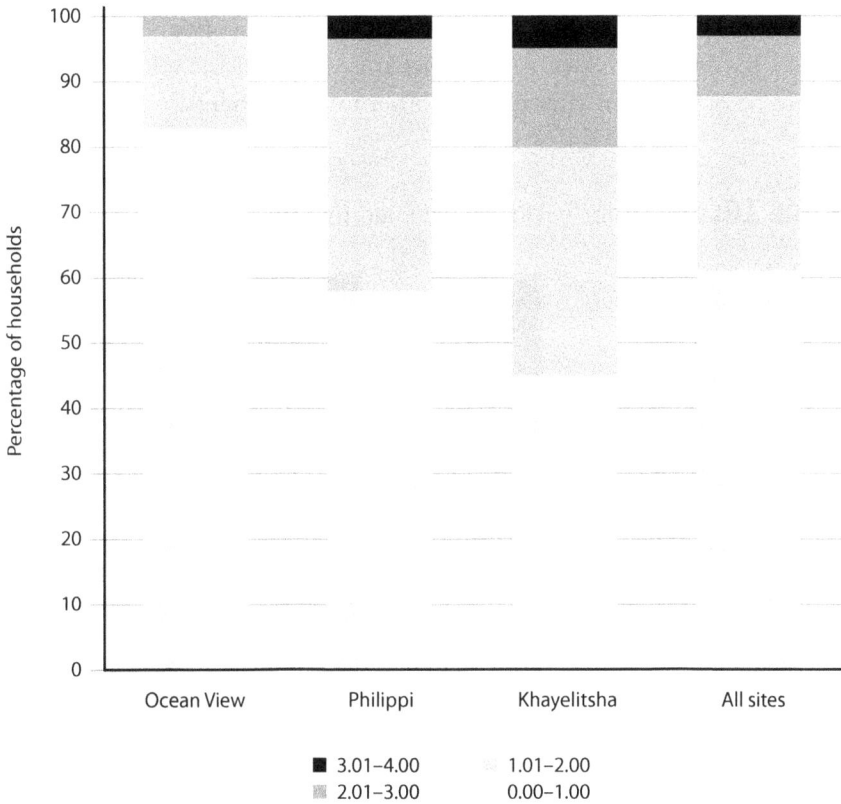

Legend:
- ■ 3.01–4.00
- 2.01–3.00
- 1.01–2.00
- 0.00–1.00

4. LEVELS OF FOOD INSECURITY IN CAPE TOWN

Levels of food insecurity proved to be extremely high in the surveyed communities. According to the Household Food Insecurity Access Scale (HFIAS), 80% of households were either moderately or severely food insecure, a figure that rose to as high as 89% in Khayelitsha (Figure 10).[25] Only 15% of households could be classified as food secure. In both Philippi and Khayelitsha, less than 10% of households were food secure. Even in Ocean View, the better-off of the three areas, only 31% of households were food secure. Dietary diversity (as measured by the HDDS) was also poor.[26] The median HDDS for food groups consumed in the previous 24 hours was 6 (out of a possible 12). While a median of 6 and a mean of 6.33 may appear relatively diverse, when the actual foodstuffs consumed are considered, it is evident that diversity was quite limited (Figure 11).

Of the four most commonly consumed foodstuffs, three are largely non-nutritive: foods made with oils/fats (consumed by 72% of households), sugar and honey (83%) and "other" (usually tea and coffee) (88%). This suggests that although the average diet may have caloric adequacy, it is likely to be deficient in vitamins and other micronutrients.

FIGURE 10: Prevalence of Household Food Insecurity

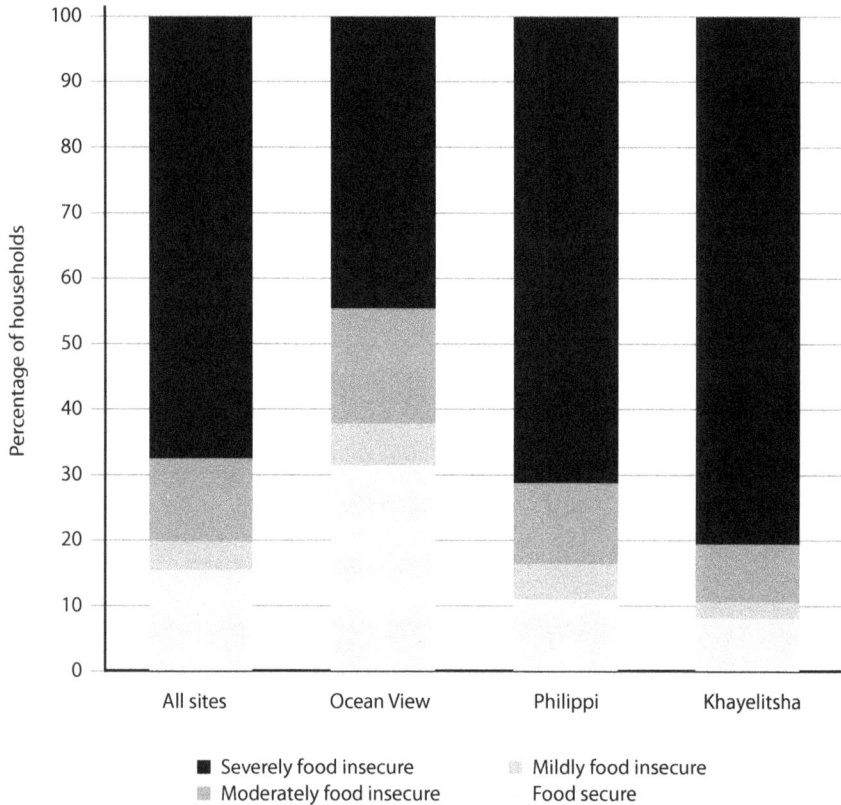

Given the South African urban tradition of eating samp and beans as a meal, it was surprising that the proportion of households eating foods made with beans, lentils, peas and other forms of non-animal derived protein was very low. These are generally low-cost, high protein foods. Among the possible reasons for this finding is the time that it takes to cook them, which in the context of high energy costs and long commutes to work makes these foods less viable. The proportion of households consuming fish was also lower than expected (only 16%) despite the fisheries history of Ocean View. While Ocean View households were more likely to have consumed fish, the difference between the Ocean View proportion and the general survey sample was only 5 percentage points. Twenty one percent of Ocean View's households had consumed fish, compared with 12% in Philippi and 16% in Khayelitsha. Very little fresh fish is consumed; most comes in the form of canned fish, particularly pilchards, which are sold extensively in retail outlets in low-income areas.

FIGURE 11: Foods Eaten in Previous Day

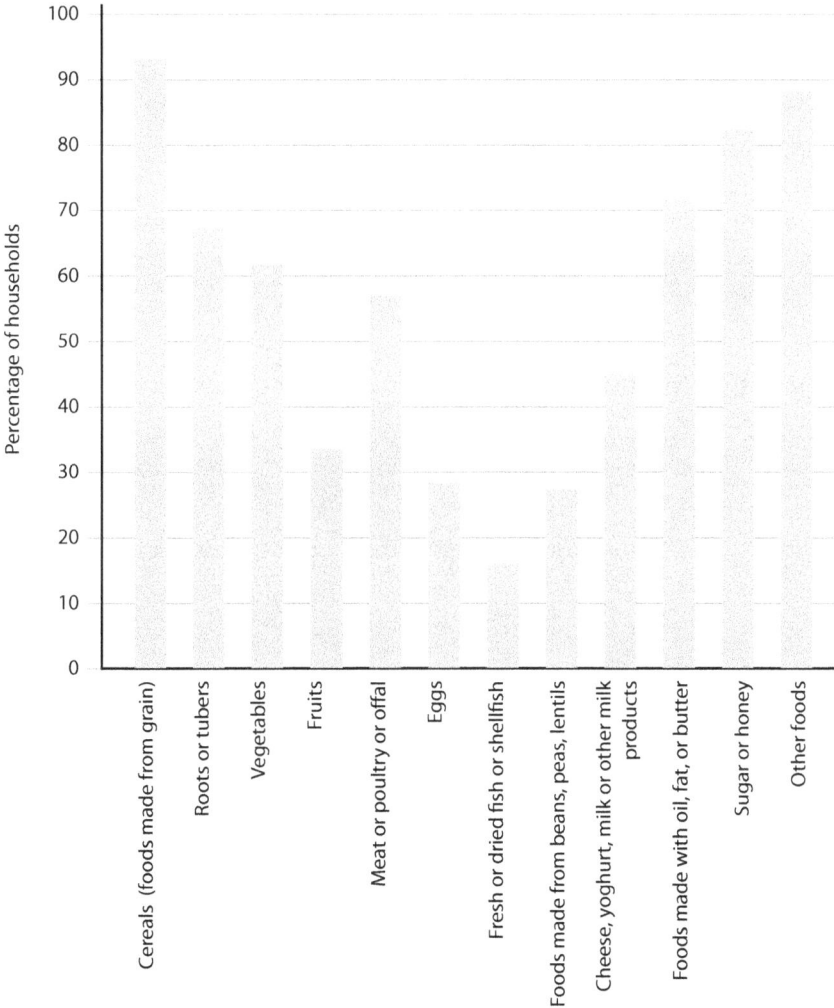

Some 88% of households stated that they had gone without food in the previous six months due to unaffordability, while 44% had gone without once a week or more. A number of respondents spoke of having "too much month for the money." In the light of this, it is unsurprising that 71% had not had enough food within the household within the previous year. The Months of Adequate Household Food Provisioning (MAHFP) score across all households was 9.2.[27] However, when food secure households were excluded, the mean fell to 8.1.

There are distinct differences in levels of food security during the year with peaks and troughs in levels of food security (Figure 12). The first trough is in January and the second in the winter, most notably June. Given the limited dependence of households on local agricultural products or food remittances from rural areas this cannot be attributed to agricultural seasonality. The January trough comes right after the December peak and is therefore related to spending cycles. Households will overspend on food over the festive season, even though their January food security is compromised. The other explanation for the trough is that many businesses (particularly the construction industry trade which employs many manual workers), close down over December and January, reducing income and casual labour opportunities. In winter (June), adverse weather conditions mean that industries employing manual labour are also less likely to operate fully or hire additional labour.

FIGURE 12: Months of Food Shortages

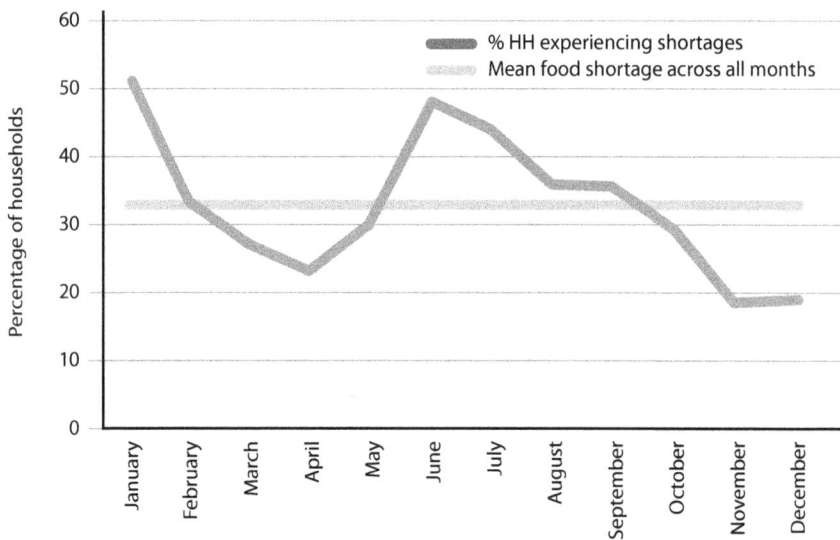

5. DETERMINANTS OF HOUSEHOLD FOOD INSECURITY

5.1 Food Insecurity and Household Structure

Rakodi suggests that the linkage between household size and household survival strategies is quite complex.[28] For example, urban households may postpone having children or send existing household members to rural areas to reduce expenditure, thus reducing or limiting household size. On the other hand, households may retain or incorporate additional members to increase income, thus increasing household size. In this survey, there does not appear to be a strong link between household size and food insecurity. Households with one to five members were actually a little more likely to be severely food insecure than those with six to 10 members (68% and 63% respectively). Similarly, there does not appear to be a strong correlation between the age of household heads and food security.

Given the gendered nature of poverty in Cape Town, female-centred households were expected to be more food insecure than other types of household.[29] And while these households were certainly the most food insecure (with 73% severely food insecure) (Figure 13), the differences with other household types were not as great as expected. Almost the same proportion of female-centred households and nuclear households were food secure, for example.

FIGURE 13: Food Security and Household Structure

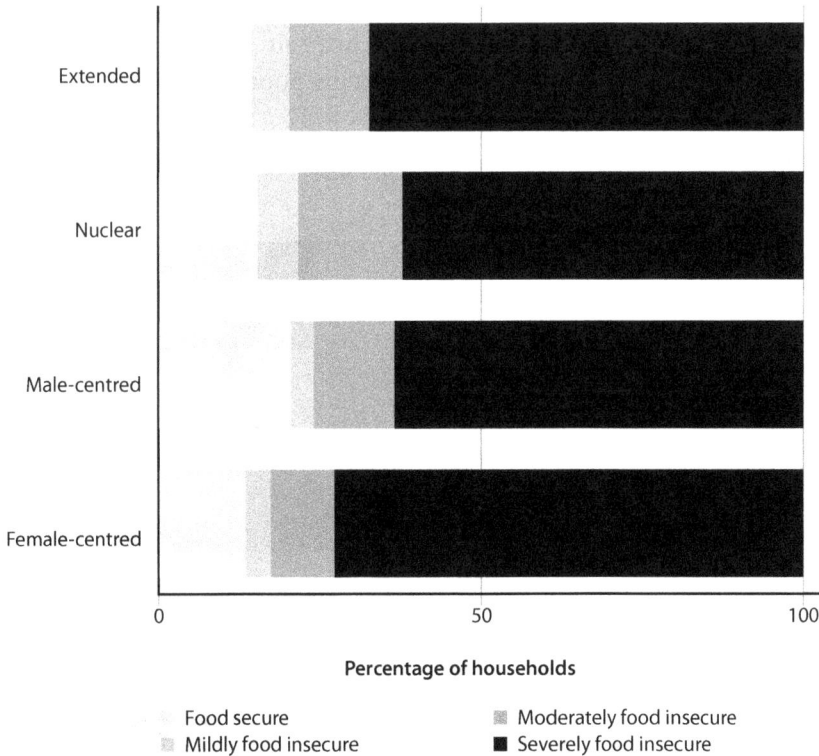

Percentage of households

Food secure   Moderately food insecure
Mildly food insecure   Severely food insecure

When household food expenditures are compared, it does not appear that female-centred households spend significantly more on food than other types of households. On average, female-centred households spend an average of 30% of their declared income on food. Nuclear households also spend 30% and extended households, 29%. Even male-centred households spend 25% of declared income on food. Part of the reason why the differences are not that dramatic may be because in all types of household where women are present, it is they that engage most in the procurement and preparation of food. The survey asked who in the household did various food related household tasks (buying, preparing, allocating, growing). The average number of food related tasks being done by females in the survey (including children) was 1.13, almost twice that of males (0.62). Females were over-represented in all food related tasks. While 56% of the sample was female, 62% of all food buying was done by women. They also do 72% of food cultivation, 75% of food preparation and 80% of food allocation.

5.2 Food Insecurity and Household Income

Urban food insecurity is often linked to levels of household income, especially within poor populations.[30] In the survey, over 80% of households in the lowest income tercile were severely food insecure. In the upper tercile, the figure was 46% (Figure 14). Households in the lowest tercile were 1.9 times more likely to be severely food insecure than those in the upper tercile. In other words, even within generally poor communities, income

FIGURE 14: Food Security Status by Income

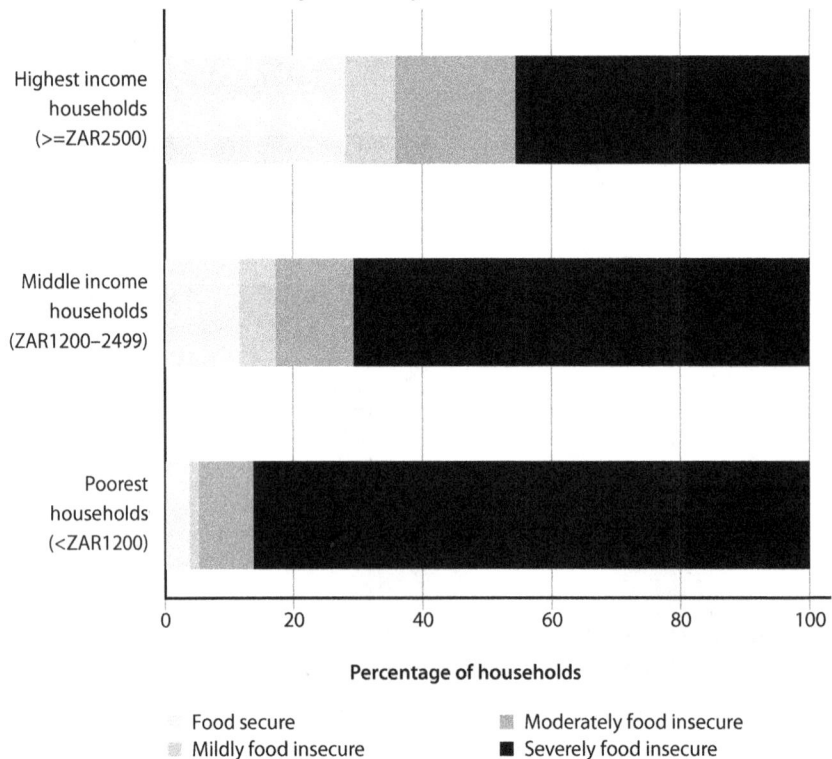

Percentage of households

Food secure
Mildly food insecure
Moderately food insecure
Severely food insecure

makes a significant difference in reducing (though not entirely elimi-
nating) food insecurity. The presence of some food insecure and food
secure households in all three terciles, however, suggests that income is
not the only determinant of food insecurity in poor communities.

Implicit in the debate on sustainable livelihoods is the assumption that
diversified livelihood strategies make households more resilient and
improve food security.[31] The survey found that food secure households
were less likely to employ additional strategies (Figure 15). The additional
livelihood profiles of severely, moderately and mildly food insecure households also looked similar, as did the profiles of lowest and highest income
tercile households (with 53% of poor households having no alternative
strategies compared with 50% in the upper tercile).

FIGURE 15: Food Security and Additional Livelihood Strategies

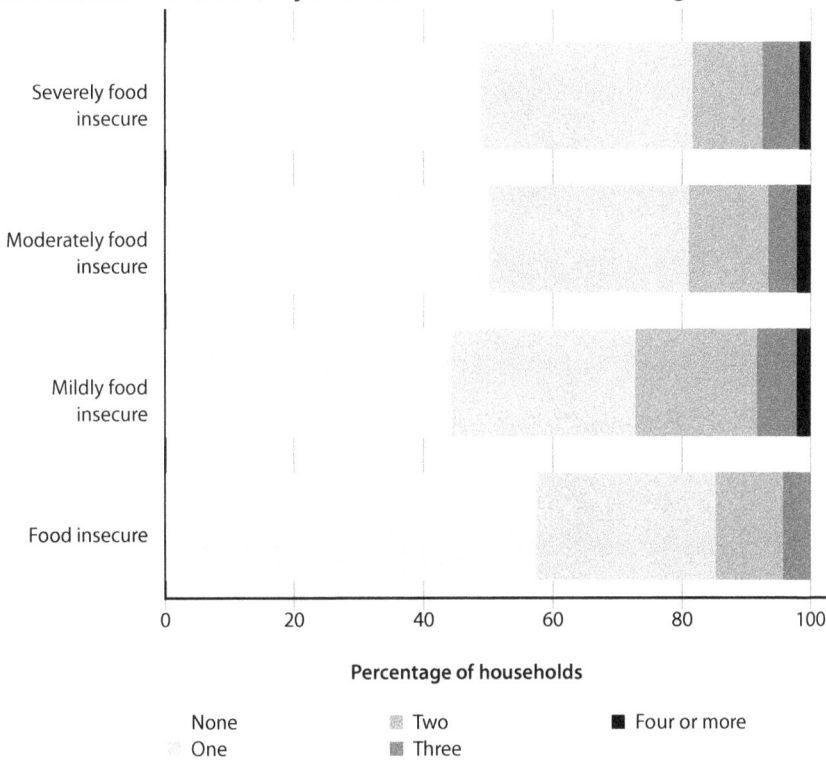

Percentage of households

None   Two   Four or more
One   Three

5.3 Food Insecurity and High Food Prices

In 2008, global and local food prices escalated rapidly.[32] In South Africa,
food inflation between October 2007 and 2008 was 16.7%, which was
4.6% higher than general inflation.[33] The majority of respondents in
the Cape Town survey indicated that their economic conditions had

worsened in the year prior to the survey (45% - much worse, 31% - worse). Only 13% said that they were the same, and 11% that they were better or much better. Households were also asked how often they had gone without enough food due to food price increases in the previous six months (Figure 16). Only 28% said they never went without due to price increases, while 35% went without about once a month, 35% more than once a week and 11% every day. The general worsening of economic conditions experienced by three-quarters of the households was largely, but not exclusively, the result of the external stress of food price increases. When households were asked to identify other factors impacting upon their ability to feed their families, 83% indicated that they had other problems including lost/reduced employment (30%), deaths, illnesses and accidents (16%) and lost/reduced income (13%).

FIGURE 16: Frequency of Going without Food

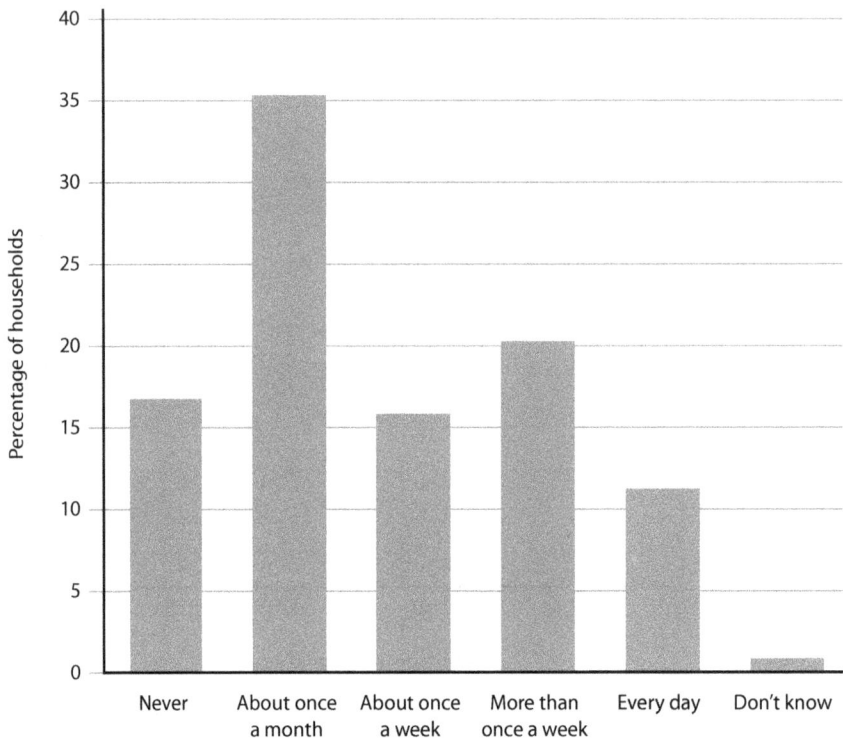

5.4 Food Insecurity and Shelter

Housing type might be expected to have direct and indirect impacts on food insecurity. For example, households with inadequate water and sanitation (the norm in many shack settlements) might be forced to eat foods that are improperly cooked or contain contaminants.[34] More indirectly, payment for shelter of some kind is a necessity and in poor households it is an expense that is often traded off against food purchase.[35] The survey found that shack dwellers were about 20 percentage points more likely to be severely food insecure than house dwellers (Figure 17). What is driving the relatively high food insecurity amongst shack dwellers? The data collected for this survey does not directly address this question. However it is likely that these households are located further from formal markets and therefore have more limited geographical access to cheaper food. They also have limited storage capacity and are therefore more likely to purchase in smaller units, which tend to be more expensive per unit volume. Further research into the role access to services (water, electricity) in food security is therefore important, as is research into the proximity to markets and storage and food preparation strategies of households.

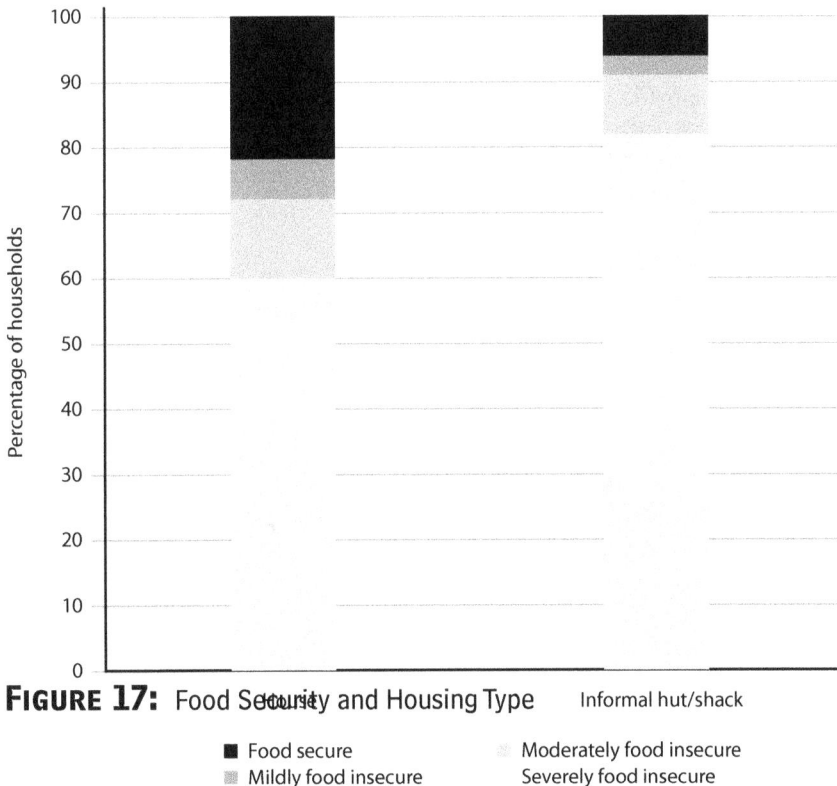

FIGURE 17: Food Security and Housing Type

■ Food secure
▦ Mildly food insecure
▒ Moderately food insecure
Severely food insecure

5.5 Food Insecurity and Urban Agriculture

Urban agriculture is increasingly being advocated as a means to reduce the food insecurity of the urban poor in Cape Town and elsewhere in

South Africa.[36] However, the AFSUN survey does not provide much encouragement to advocates of urban agriculture. Very few of the poor urban households in this survey engaged in any form of urban agriculture (field crops, garden crops, tree crops or livestock). Even the proximity of the Philippi Horticultural Area and Abalimi Bezekhaya, an urban agriculture NGO, to Brown's Farm (Ward 34) does not appear to have made a great impact. Only 4% of the households in Ward 34 said they engaged in any form of urban agriculture. This was even lower than in Ocean View (9%), but more than in Khayelitsha (less than 2%). Household urban agriculture is therefore not a significant source of food in Cape Town, despite the existence of an Urban Agriculture Policy created by the city.[37]

5.6 Food Insecurity and Social Protection

Social protection is increasingly advocated as a means to reduce food insecurity.[38] South Africa has an increasingly well-developed and inclusive set of social grants.[39] However, when the food security status of grant-receiving households in Cape Town is compared to the overall food security profile of the sample population, there is a minimal difference (Figure 18). Either grants are extraordinarily well targeted, raising the most vulnerable to a food security status comparable with non-grant

FIGURE 18: Food Security and Social Grants

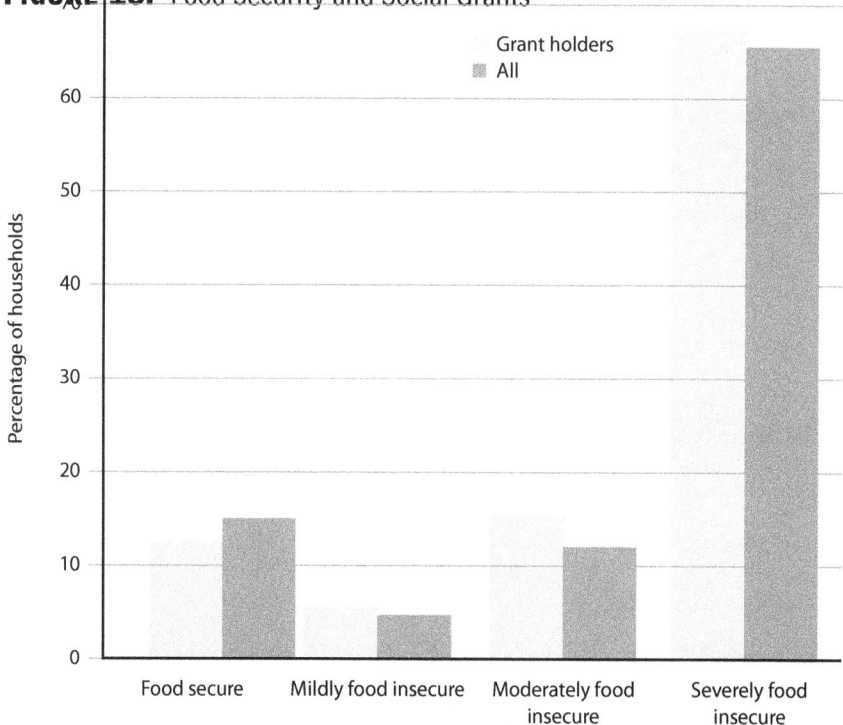

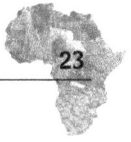

holders, or they make a minimal impact on household food security. At the time of the survey, the monthly child support grant was R220 and the old age pension, R940. It is unlikely that transfers of such relatively small amounts would make a significant difference to household food security. This would be consistent with Devereux's observation:

> Tiny transfers equal tiny impacts, but moderate transfers can have major impacts. The poor use incremental income to satisfy basic consumption needs first, then to invest in human capital (education, health) and in social capital (supporting others, but also building up the basis for reciprocal claims), and finally to invest in directly productive (income-generating) assets and livelihood activities. Income transfers will impact on productive investment only if they are large enough also to cover immediate consumption needs.[40]

5.7 Food Insecurity and Migration

Two-thirds of the surveyed population had migrated at some point during their lives. The most common reasons given for migration were economic (37%), family (22%, most commonly moving with family), living conditions (18%) and education (14%). The heavy presence of economic migrants in these urban households suggested that they would be significant remitters to areas outside the city. However, very few households recognised themselves as migrant households or had remittance-based relationships with relatives in rural areas. Only 77 households (less than 10% of the total sample) included remittances as part of their household expenditure profile. The median remittance amount was R1 000 per month. This suggests that although there are many migrants within the city, the linkages between these migrants and their sending households are not financially significant.

In some African cities rural to urban transfers of cash and food are significant for poor urban households.[41] In the Cape Town survey, only 52 households said they received remittances in cash, 10 in goods and 28 in food (less than 10% in total). The mean income or value derived from cash remittances was R402 per month, R424 from goods and R498 from food. However, when these figures are disaggregated, it becomes apparent that these households are more dependent on urban to urban than rural to urban transfers. Although the numbers are small, such transfers are more prevalent in food insecure than food secure households.

6. The Geography of Food Access in Cape Town

Household food security is determined in part by the geography of the city which influences the range of livelihood strategies households are able to employ. These spatial challenges are reinforced or mitigated by governance decisions taken by the City of Cape Town, particularly with regard to the regulation of the informal sector and zoning. The first spatial element is the physical location of households which impacts on food security by shaping the resources they are able to draw on to purchase food or obtain it from alternative sources.[42]

The second spatial element is the actual food geography of the city. The location of markets (formal and informal) and other sources of food interact with the personal geographies of households to impact upon food security. In other words, households may have adequate resources to access food, but their location relative to accessible, affordable food may render them food insecure. The work of others on food geographies in North America and Britain has highlighted the confluence of spatial and economic exclusion from the food system leading to what have been termed "food deserts."[43] These are defined as "areas of relative exclusion where people experience physical and economic barriers to accessing healthy food."[44]

Poor households in Cape Town access food in three main ways: through food purchase (from both formal and informal outlets), through formal social safety nets, and through social networks (Figure 19). As indicated above, very few households (less than 5%) obtain food by growing it themselves. The dominant source of purchased food in all of the three study sites turned out to be supermarkets (patronised by 94% of all households in the previous year), followed by small shops, restaurants and "take-aways" (75%) and informal markets or street food sellers (66%).

Although more households purchase food at supermarkets, daily and weekly purchases are far more likely to be made at small shops or from informal outlets. The majority of households said they only purchase food from supermarkets once a month which could be a function of accessibility or because supermarkets are used to purchase only certain kinds of (bulk) items or because households only have sufficient disposable income to patronise supermarkets on paydays.

Patronage of the informal food economy is shaped by high transport costs, a lack of money to make bulk purchases and concerns about the safety of routes near supermarkets. Supermarkets tend to be located on busy intersections to maximise the potential number of shoppers using the store, but research in Philippi has identified that these intersections are also associated with high opportunistic crime.[45] On the other hand, reliance on informal food sources can increase the unit cost of foodstuffs, reduce access to high quality foods and increase the health risks from unsanitary conditions of food preparation and storage.[46]

FIGURE 19: Sources of Food

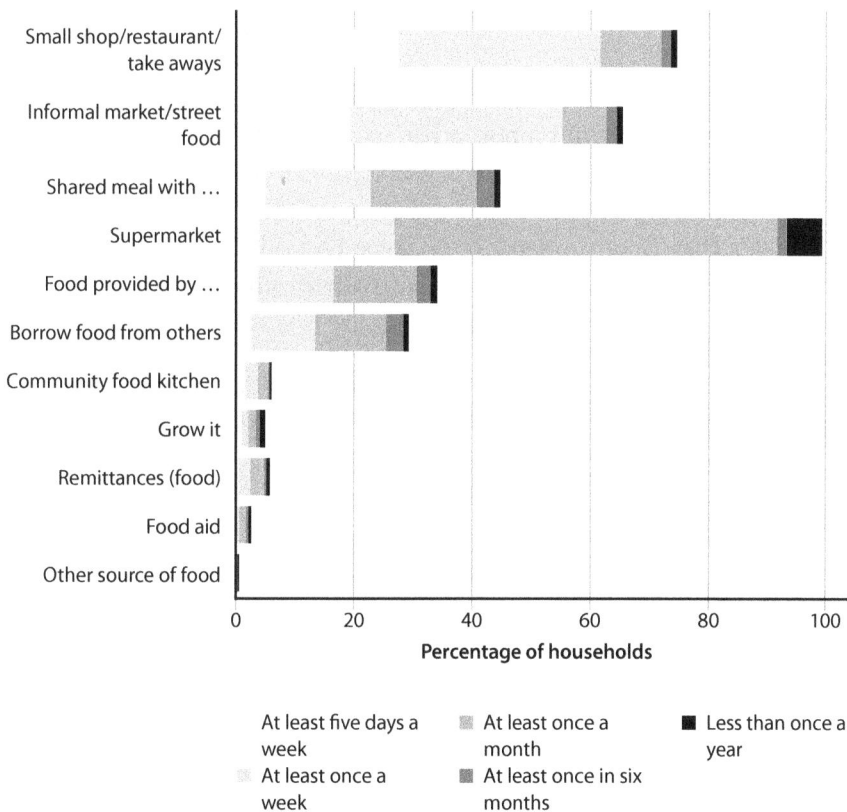

A significant number of households had acquired food from neighbours and other households through sharing meals (44% in the previous year), eating food provided by others (34%) and borrowing food (29%). A smaller number received food in the form of remittances from outside the city (6%). This all points to the existence of strong social networks within the poor areas of Cape Town. However, it also suggests that many of the urban poor are unable to access enough food through the market and have to depend on these informal networks for survival. The extensive borrowing from the urban poor by the urban poor potentially reduces general household resilience. The sharing and borrowing of food can mask the extent of food insecurity amongst the urban poor and obscure the failings of formal urban food systems. A very small proportion of surveyed households had accessed food directly through formal safety nets. Just 6% used community food kitchens and 3% food aid. In the context of the high levels of food insecurity within the city, the minor role of formal social safety nets in household food security and the pressure informal safety nets place on already vulnerable households is highly problematic.

7. ILLNESS AND FOOD INSECURITY

Previous studies have identified a close connection between poverty and ill-health in Cape Town's poor urban communities.[47] In this survey, almost a quarter of the households reported that a household member had been ill in the past year, and 7% that a household member had died. Households that were moderately or severely food insecure were more likely to have had a household member with an illness than those who were food secure or only mildly food insecure (Figure 20).

FIGURE 20: Food Security and Household Experience of Illness or Death

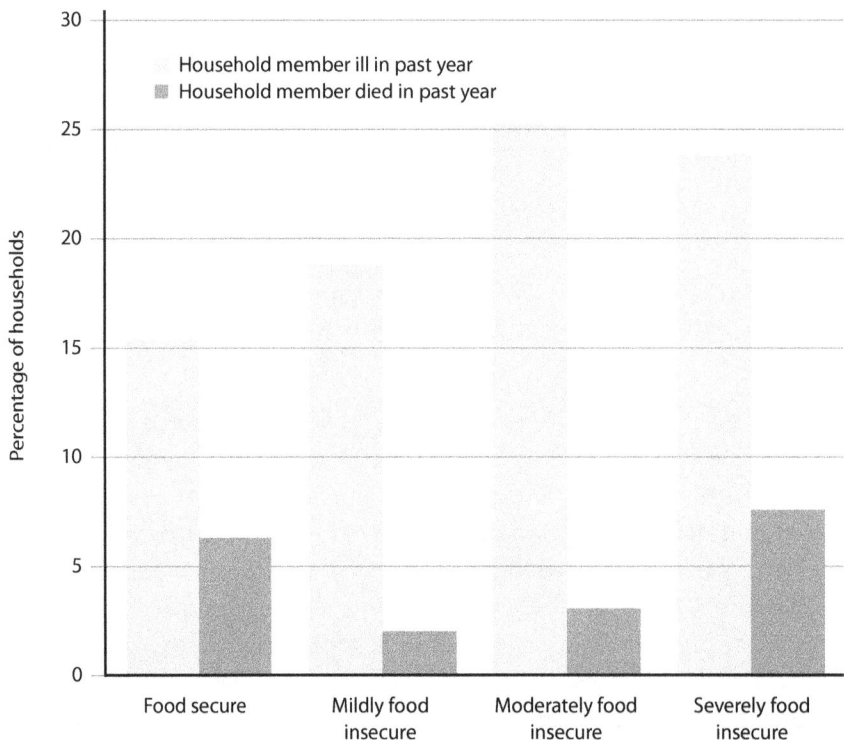

However, household member deaths did not appear to correlate to food insecurity. It is difficult to draw a causal link between morbidity and food security. Are the food insecure households more likely to have illnesses because of their food security status, or does illness increase the risk of food insecurity? The literature suggests a bi-directional relationship.[48]

Respondents identified the existence of a wide range of illnesses (Figure 21). Recognising the stigma attached to HIV and AIDS, the proxies of TB and pneumonia were included in the survey.[49] Of the 22% of households with ill members, a third identified HIV and AIDS or TB or pneumonia (i.e. around 7% in all). While these represent a significant proportion of all reported illnesses, they also suggest under-reporting of HIV and AIDS prevalence. In 2005, for example, Cape Town had an HIV prevalence rate of 15.7%, with the Khayelitsha health district having a prevalence rate of 27.2%.[50]

FIGURE 21: Reported Illnesses

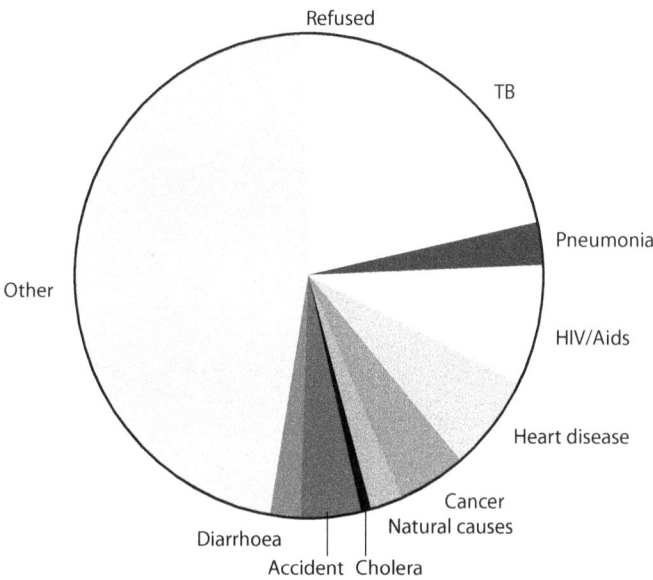

Of those who had had an illness in the previous year, 25% were making contributions to household income through work. Many of these ill household members probably had reduced income due to their inability to work, thus affecting food security. Of those who had died in the past year, 60% had been making some form of contribution to household income (29% through work and 32% through grants). Clearly these illnesses and deaths represent a reduction in income for households, thus increasing their vulnerability to food insecurity.

The household members most likely to be have been ill were household heads (28%) and sons or daughters (27%). Household heads are likely to be the main sources of income in the household. Older children may provide a secondary income source. Compromised health of younger children may impact upon their long term physical and mental development, thus impacting their future food security. Older members of the sample population were also more likely to have been ill than younger ones (Figure 22). This is due both to the general age profile of chronic diseases, such as hypertension and diabetes, and the under-reporting of asymptomatic diseases, in particular HIV.

FIGURE 22: Age of Ill Household Members Compared to Entire Sample

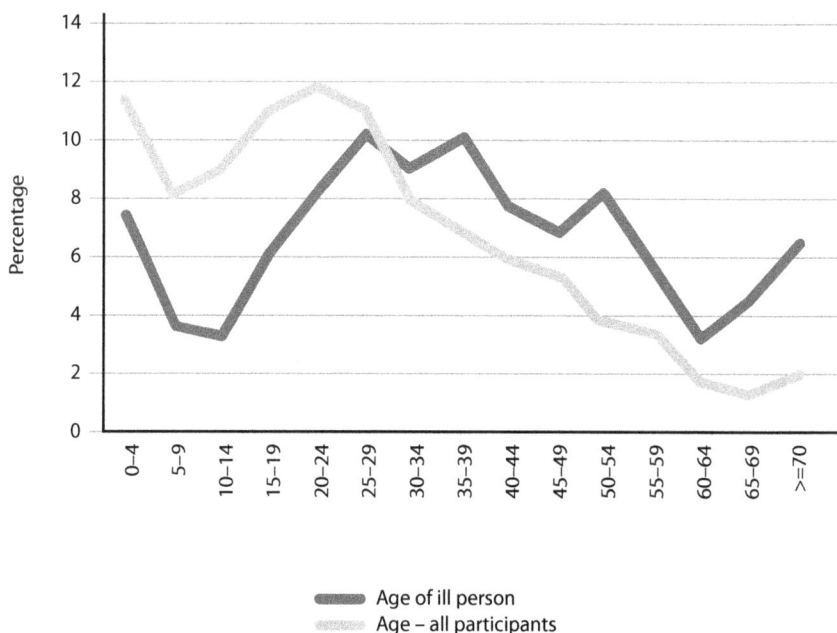

Age of ill person
Age – all participants

8. CONCLUSION

Food insecurity in the poor areas of Cape Town is both severe and chronic. Even in the most food secure site sampled, Ocean View, just 31% of the households could be considered to be food secure. The evidence indicates that food security is worsening in poor areas of the city with 76% of households indicating that their economic circumstances were either much worse or worse than a year previously. In the light of the current global economic crisis and local challenges, such as rapidly increasing food and electricity prices, as well as persistent joblessness and skills shortages,

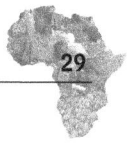

it is likely that growing numbers of households will experience food insecurity. Households will reduce their food intake, reduce the range of foods they eat and substitute 'good' foods with cheaper, nutritionally inferior foods. These food choices may have long term health and human development outcomes. In addition, in order to reduce food security, households will possibly adopt survival strategies that could be to their long-term detriment. These strategies may include reducing women's and children's portion sizes, removing children from school, and working in hazardous environments or in unsafe industries.

In choosing three different and widely scattered sites for the survey, it was anticipated that there would be considerable intra-city variation in levels and determinants of food insecurity. Ocean View was generally less poor and food insecure than the other two sites. The mean household income of Ocean View was more than twice that of the wards in Philippi and Khayelitsha. The prevalence and depth of food security was higher in the latter than in Ocean View. However, even there, levels of food insecurity were extremely high with 62% of households being either severely or moderately food insecure. Despite its relative wealth, 47% of Ocean View's households were still below the City of Cape Town's indigency line. The proportion of food insecure households in Philippi and Khayelitsha was 84% and 89% respectively. Despite some differences, what was striking was the similarities between the three sites. These particular sites were selected in order to capture a range of different household strategies to access food, yet these local differences proved to be of minor importance.

Food security is generally viewed as closely related to poverty. The survey data supports this general finding. Likewise, when food security is mapped onto income terciles, those in the lowest income tercile were almost twice as likely to fall into the severely food insecure category as those in the highest income tercile. However, households at all food security levels were present in all income categories. Although income is a good predictor of food security, the relationship is not perfect. Nearly all food insecure households are poor but not all households in poor communities are food insecure. The survey suggests that there is a need for a more nuanced approach to poverty and its relationship to food insecurity. Finally, it is important to note that poverty is not just experienced, but also responded to. A livelihoods approach which considers the range and extent of household resources and their food security strategies is useful for understanding the dynamic link between food security and poverty.

The data presented on sources of food highlights that food access is not simply determined by adequacy of income and other household-scale

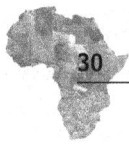

characteristics, but also by physical access to markets. Research and poli-cies aimed at addressing urban food security need to engage beyond the conventional household scale and examine the spatial and structural factors impacting food security. Northern research on food deserts provides a valuable starting point for such an approach, with the more recent literature by beginning to connect household and spatial determi-nants of food insecurity.[51] However, while this approach is useful it should not be uncritically replicated in the Southern African context given its assumption that food purchasing behaviours are largely local (when many households purchase food on journeys from work), and the continued importance of both informal food retail and informal social safety nets as sources of food.

The findings from the field reinforce the fact that in the urban setting, there are multiple causes of food insecurity. There is also a range of stake-holders playing a role in the urban food system. As a result, the solution to food insecurity cannot simply be linked to local and national policy interventions. The findings on food sources, in particular, suggest a failure in the current food market. The state and private sector will need to work together to address some of the weaknesses of the current food distribution and sales systems. The informal food economy is a vitally important means for people to access food. In policy terms, enhancement of the informal market as a means of food supply is vital.[52] Furthermore, considerable strain is being placed on community resources as households borrow and share food. While this suggests strong social capital in the poor areas of the city, it also points to a failure of the market and of formal social safety nets.

A related policy theme is therefore that engagement between NGOs, civil society and the state should be encouraged in order to put in place safety nets that neither create dependency nor destroy existing social safety nets which perpetuate community relations. The city therefore needs to develop a food security strategy that goes beyond a focus on produc-tion and absolute supply. This strategy must consider supply chains, procurement, nutrition support programmes, public health, environ-mental sustainability, water and waste, and the support of local enterprise amongst others. Furthermore, it must consider the geography of the urban food system, in particular planning and zoning regulations regarding the location of both formal and informal retail within low income areas of the city. At the core, there are two elements to consider with regard to household food security. The first is to develop strategies that facilitate sustainable economic opportunities for households to move out of food insecurity. The second is to develop appropriate safety nets for those who will be not be able to harness these opportunities. In order to achieve

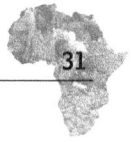

these macro-objectives, it will be important to develop an understanding not just about the experience of poor people in the city, but also what it is about the city that produces food insecurity. Why, for example, do residents of Cape Town have so few livelihood strategies despite their high food insecurity? Ultimately, the policy and governance focus should be to plan for a food secure city and make food central to all city-planning processes.

This survey has provided a good baseline understanding of the nature of urban food security in Cape Town. Two general areas of future research can be identified. Firstly, research to understand urban food security needs to begin at the household scale and map household food geographies in order to develop a deeper understanding of the spatial and non-spatial determinants of food insecurity. Secondly, in order to address the policy questions raised, it will be vital to conduct further research into the nature and governance of the city and the impact of this on food security. It would allow analysis to be conducted beyond the neighbourhood scale and for connections between food system and other inequities to be acknowledged.

ENDNOTES

1   Statistics South Africa, *Community Survey 2007: Basic Results: Municipalities* (Pretoria, Statistics South Africa, 2008), p. 18.

2   C. Mieklejohn and S. le Roux, *A National Overview of Spatial Trends and Settlement Characteristics: Annexure A, Population Characteristics and Location.* (Pretoria: CSIR, 2008).

3   J. Erasmus, S. Francis, P. Kok, B. Roberts, C. Schwabe and A. Todes, *State of the Cities Report 2006* (Johannesburg: South African Cities Network, 2006), p. 37.

4   City of Cape Town, *State of Cape Town 2006: Development Issues in Cape Town* (Cape Town, 2006), p. 25.

5   D. McDonald, *World City Syndrome: Neoliberalism and Inequality in Cape Town* (New York: Routledge, 2008).

6   W. Crane and M. Swilling "Environment, Sustainable Resource Use and the Cape Town Functional Region – An Overview" *Urban Forum* 19(3) (2008): 263-87; A. Sebitosi, "Energy Efficiency, Security of Supply and the Environment in South Africa: Moving Beyond the Strategy Documents" *Energy* 33(11), 2008, 1591-6; B. Büscher, "Connecting Political Economies of Energy in South Africa" *Energy Policy* 37(10) (2009): 3951-8; G. Ziervogel, M. Shale and M. Du, "Climate Change Adaptation in a Developing Country Context: The Case of Urban Water Supply in Cape Town" *Climate and Development* 2(2) (2010): 94-110.

7   C. de Swardt, T. Puoane, M. Chopra and A. du Toit, "Urban Poverty in Cape Town." *Environment and Urbanization* 17(2) (2005):101-11.

8   A. Misselhorn, "What Drives Food Insecurity in Southern Africa? A Meta-

Analysis of Household Economy Studies" *Global Environmental Change Part A* 15(1) (2005): 33-43; F. Wenhold, M. Faber, W. van Averbeke, A. Oelofse, P. van Jaarsveld, W. Jansen van Rensburg, I. van Heerden and R Slabbert, "Linking Smallholder Agriculture and Water to Household Food Security and Nutrition" *Water SA* 33(3) (2007): 327-36; C. Valente, "The Food (In)Security Impact of Land Redistribution in South Africa: Microeconometric Evidence from National Data" *World Development* 37(9) (2009): 1540-53; E. Kimani-Murage,K. Kahn,J. Pettifor, S. Tollman, D. Dunger,X. Gómez-Olivé and S. Norris, "The Prevalence of Stunting, Overweight and Obesity, and Metabolic Disease Risk in Rural South African Children" *BMC Public Health* 10 (2010): 158; M. Faber, C. Witten, S. Drimie, "Community-Based Agricultural Interventions in the Context of Food and Nutrition Security in South Africa" *South African Journal of Clinical Nutrition* 24(1) (2011): 21-30.

9   J. Crush and B. Frayne, *The Invisible Crisis: Urban Food Security in Southern Africa*, AFSUN Series No 1, Cape Town, 2010.

10   M. McLachlan and J. Thorne, "Seeding Change: A Proposal for Renewal in the South African Food System" Development Planning Division Working Paper Series No 16, Development Bank of Southern Africa, Midrand, 2009.

11   A. Todes, P. Kok, M. Wentzel, J. Van Zyl and C. Cross, "Contemporary South African Urbanization Dynamics" *Urban Forum* 21(3) (2010):331-348.

12   Section 27(1)(b) of the South African Constitution states that "everyone has the right to have access to sufficient food and water"; see Constitution of the Republic of South Africa No 108 of 1996 at http://www.info.gov.za/documents/constitution/1996/a108-96.pdf

13   World Food Programme, *World Hunger Series 2007: Hunger and Health* (Rome, 2007).

14   See http://www.afsun.org

15   J. Crush and B. Frayne, *The State of Urban Food Security in Southern Africa*. AFSUN Series No. 2, Cape Town, 2010.

16   J. Coates, A. Swindale and P. Bilinsky, *Household Food Insecurity Access Scale (HFIAS) for Measurement of Food Access: Indicator Guide (Version 3)* (Washington, DC: Food and Nutrition Technical Assistance Project, Academy for Educational Development: 2007), pp.18; A. Swindale and P. Bilinsky, *Household Dietary Diversity Score (HDDS) for Measurement of Household Food Access: Indicator Guide (Version 2)* (Washington, DC: Food and Nutrition Technical Assistance Project, Academy for Educational Development, 2006); P. Bilinsky and A. Swindale, *Months of Adequate Household Food Provisioning (MAHFP) for Measurement of Household Food Access: Indicator Guide* (Washington, DC: Food and Nutrition Technical Assistance Project, Academy for Educational Development, 2007).

17   Municipal Development Partnership for Eastern and Southern Africa (MDPESA), *Situational Analysis for RUAF/Philippi Urban Agriculture Project* (MDPESA: Harare, 2008) at http://www.mdpafrica.org.zw/index.php?option=com_content&view=article&id=48&Itemid=1

18   B. Frayne, "Pathways of Food: Migration and Food Security in Southern African Cities." *International Development Planning Review* 32(3/4) (2010):83-104

19   A. Dorward, S.Anderson ,Y. Nava, J.Pattison, R.Paz, J.Rushton and E.Sanchez Vera, "Hanging In, Stepping up and Stepping Out: Livelihood Aspirations and Strategies of the Poor" *Development in Practice* 19(2) (2009): 240-7.

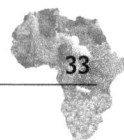

20   Western Cape Provincial Government (Provincial Treasury), "Regional Development Profile: City of Cape Town," Working Paper, Cape Town, 2010, p. 16.

21   City of Cape Town, *City's Indigent Policy* (2008) at http://www.capetown.gov.za/ en/Pages/Indigentpolicy.aspx

22   See S. Chant, "Female Household Headship and Feminisation of Poverty: Facts, Fictions and Forward Policies." New Working Paper Series 9, London School of Economics, Gender Institute, LSE, London, 2003.

23   R. Mattes, "The Material and Political Bases of Lived Poverty in Africa" Afrobarometer Working Paper 98, Idasa, Cape Town, 2008.

24   Ibid., p. 11.

25   Coates et al, *Household Food Insecurity Access Scale (HFIAS)*.

26   Swindale and Bilinsky, *Household Dietary Diversity Score (HDDS)*.

27   Bilinsky and Swindale, *Months of Adequate Household Food Provisioning (MAHFP)*.

28   C. Rakodi, "A Capital Assets Framework for Analysing Household Livelihood Strategies: Implications for Policy" *Development Policy Review* 17(3) (1999), p. 320.

29   R. Slater, "Urban Agriculture, Gender and Empowerment: An Alternative View" *Development Southern Africa* 18(5) (2001):635-50.

30   D. Maxwell, "The Political Economy of Urban Food Security in Sub-Saharan Africa" *World Development* 27(11) (1999): 1939-53; M. Cohen and J. Garratt, "The Food Price Crisis and Urban Food (In)security" *Environment and Urbanization* 22 (2010): 467-82.

31   S. Maxwell, "Food Security: A Postmodern Perspective" *Food Policy* 21(2) (1996):155-70; S. Sallu, C. Twyman and L. Stringer, "Resilient or Vulnerable Livelihoods? Assessing Livelihood Dynamics and Trajectories in Rural Botswana" *Ecology and Society* 15(4) (2010); FAO "Best Practices to Support and Improve the Livelihoods of Small-Scale Fisheries and Aquatic Households" RAP Publication 2010/21,Regional Office for Asia and the Pacific (2010).

32   J. Garrett, C. Hawkes and M. Cohen. "The Food, Fuel, and Financial Crises Affect the Urban and Rural Poor Disproportionately: A Review of the Evidence" *The Journal of Nutrition* 140(1) (2010):170-6; I. Darton-Hill, "Maternal and Young Child Nutrition Adversely Affected by External Shocks Such As Increasing Global Food Prices" *The Journal of Nutrition* 140(1) (2010):162-9; Cohen and Garratt, "The Food Price Crisis and Urban Food (In)security."

33   National Agricultural Marketing Council (NAMC), *Food Price Monitor, November, 2008*.

34   T. Govender, J. Barnes and C. Pieper, "Housing Conditions, Sanitation Status and Associated Health Risks in Selected Subsidized Low-Cost Housing Settlements in Cape Town, South Africa" *Habitat International* 35 (2001): 335-42.

35   T. Govender, J. Barnes and C. Pieper, "The Impact of Densification by Means of Informal Shacks in the Backyards of Low-Cost Houses on the Environment and Service Delivery in Cape Town, South Africa" *Environmental Health Insights* 5(2011): 23-52.

36   S. Reuther and N. Dewar, "Competition for the Use of Public Open Space in Low-Income Urban Areas: The Economic Potential of Urban Gardening in Khayelitsha, Cape Town" *Development Southern Africa* 23(1) (2006):97-122; C. Rogerson, "Resetting the Policy Agenda for Urban Agriculture in South Africa"

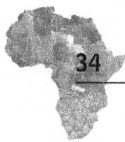

Journal of Public Administration 45(2) (2010):373-383; N. Webb, "When is Enough, Enough? Advocacy, Evidence and Criticism in the Field of Urban Agriculture in South Africa" *Development Southern Africa* 28(2) (2011):195-208; J. Crush, A. Hovorka and D. Tevera, *Urban Food Production and Household Food Security in Southern African Cities*, AFSUN Series No. 4, Cape Town, 2010.

37   City of Cape Town (2007) *Urban Agriculture Policy for the City of Cape Town*, City of Cape Town: Cape Town.

38   A. Barrientos and D. Hulme, eds., *Social Protection for the Poor and Poorest* (London: Palgrave Macmillan, 2008); F. Ellis, S. Devereux and P. White, *Social Protection in Africa* (Cheltenham: Edward Elgar, 2009).

39   A. Barrientos and J. DeJong, "Reducing Child Poverty with Cash Transfers: A Sure Thing?" *Development Policy Review* 24(5) (2006):537-52; K. Pauw and L. Mncube, "Expanding the Social Security Net in South Africa: Opportunities, Challenges and Constraints" UNDP International Poverty Centre (IPC), Country Study No 8, 2007; F. Lund, *Changing Social Policy: The Child Support Grant in South Africa* (Pretoria: HSRC Press, 2008).

40   S. Devereux, "Can Social Safety Nets Reduce Chronic Poverty?" *Development Policy Review* 20(5) (2002):672-3.

41   Frayne, "Pathways of Food."

42   S. Zenk, A. Shutz, B. Israel, S. James, S. Bao and M. Wilson, "Neighborhood Composition, Neighbourhood Poverty, and the Spatial Accessibility of Supermarkets in Detroit" *American Journal of Public Health* 95(4) (2005): 660-7.

43   C. Reisig and A. Hobbiss, "Food Deserts and How to Tackle Them: A Study of One City's Approach" *Health Education Journal* 59 (2000): 137-149; N. Wrigley, "Food Deserts in British Cities: Policy Context and Research Priorities" *Urban Studies* 39(11) (2002): 2029-40; N. Wrigley, D. Warm and B. Margetts, "Deprivation, Diet, and Food-Retail Access: Findings from the Leeds 'Food Deserts' Study" *Environment and Planning A* 35(1) (2003):151-88; H. Shaw, "Food Deserts: Towards the Development of a Classification" *GeografiskerAnnaler Series B*: Human Geography 88B(2) (2006): 231-47; P. Apparicio, M-S. Cloutier and R. Shearmur, "The Case of Montréal's Missing Food Deserts: Evaluation of Accessibility to Food Supermarkets" *International Journal of Health Geographics* 6:4 (2007); A. Short, J. Guthman and S. Raskin, "Food Deserts, Oases, or Mirages?" *Journal of Planning Education and Research* 26(3) (2007): 352-64; S. Raja, C. Ma and P. Yadav, "Beyond Food Deserts: Measuring and Mapping Racial Disparities in Neighborhood Food Environments" *Journal of Planning Education and Research* 27 (2008).

44   Reisig and Hobbis, "Food Deserts" p. 138.

45   Personal Communication from Gita Goven, 2009.

46   J. Crush, B. Frayne and M. McLachlan, *Rapid Urbanization and the Nutrition Transition in Southern Africa*, AFSUN Series No. 7, Cape Town, 2011.

47   D. Ndegwa, D. Horner and F. Esau, "The Links between Migration, Poverty and Health: Evidence for Khayelitsha and Mitchell's Plain" *Social Indicators Research* 81(2) (2007):223-234; J. Skordis-Worrall, K. Hanson and A. Mills, "Estimating the Demand for Health Services in Four Poor Districts of Cape Town, South Africa" *International Health* 3(1) (2011):44-49.; T. Govender, J. Barnes and C. Pieper, "Living in Low-Cost Housing Settlements in Cape Town, South

Africa – The Epidemiological Characteristics Associated with Increased Health Vulnerability" *Journal of Urban Health* 87(6) (2010):899-911.

48   WFP, *World Hunger Series* 2006.

49   S. Kalichman and L. Simbayi, "HIV Testing Attitudes, AIDS Stigma, and Voluntary HIV Counselling and Testing in a Black Township in Cape Town, South Africa" *Sexually Transmitted Infections* 79(6) (2003):442-47.

50   City of Cape Town, *State of Cape Town 2006*, p. 33.

51   Shaw, "Food Deserts"; C. Cannuscio, E. Weiss and D. Asch, "The Contribution of Urban Foodways to Health Disparities" *Journal of Urban Health: Bulletin of the New York Academy of Medicine* 87(3) (2010): 381-93.

52   J. Battersby, "Urban Food Insecurity in Cape Town, An Alternative Approach to Food Access" *Development Southern Africa* 28(4) (2011): 545-61.

www.ingramcontent.com/pod-product-compliance
Lightning Source LLC
Chambersburg PA
CBHW080135270326
41926CB00021B/4494